PRINTHOUSE BOOKS PRESENTS

Beautiful Strange: Memoirs of a Life Once Lived

Kalandra St. George

VIP INK Publishing Group, Inc.

Atlanta, GA.

Beautiful Strange: Memoirs of a Life
Once Lived

Kalandra St. George

Beautiful Strange

Beautiful Strange:
Memoirs of a Life Once Lived
ISBN:978-0-997-8116-98
Editor: Tarsha Gray

Published by:
VIP INK Publishing Group, Inc.
PRINTHOUSE BOOKS
Atlanta, Georgia
www.printhousebooks.com

Cover Art by: SK7

LCCN:2017932503

Printed in the United States of America

i stomp through the recesses of my mind

like the giant come down off the beanstalk of Jack

and what do i find???

destruction

destruction everywhere...

kalandrayvonne

Beautiful Strange

Table of Contents

Beautiful Strange . . .8

Jackals In The Night . . .10

Celibacy. . . .13

Tears 17

Moonmilk 20

Southpaw 22

Relativity 23

Tennessee 28

Satin Sheets 30

Gentleman's Jack 32

Kalandra St. George

Table of Contents

Lamentations: A Series

     Vamping . . .34

     White Liquor . . . 34

     Lyrics . . .35

The Crow and The Butterfly 37

I Am Life 40

Knowledge 42

My People 44

About the Author . . .46

Contact the Author . . .48

Beautiful Strange

Beautiful Strange: Memoirs of a Life Once Lived is a vivid compilation of poetry and prose that beautifully depicts the life of novelist and poet Kalandra St. George. As it trundles fluidly through a vast landscape of emotions, Beautiful chronicles a lifetime of love, resentment, self-doubt, and revelation. It embodies all of the elements of the human mind in a time of struggle, wonder, and constant inquiry, told through a soulful collection of prose. St. George lays bare her deepest thoughts and secrets to her readers through the vivid language of poetry.

...and although each time i was left less than before there always seemed to be more beauty a hellious beacon whose only purpose was to attract prowlers continuously to my tomb so here i lay lifeless and desecrated exposed and hopeless looted and plundered shattered and torn exhausted and angry ashamed and confused but still oh so Beautiful -Jackals In the Night

Beautiful Strange

i came from a broken heart

so it's no surprise mine remains in pieces

pieces of him that weren't enough for her fragile

psyche

so he gave her what he could

and she reluctantly accepted

gathering him into her womb

molding the delicate cells into clumps of flesh

that would birth a fragmented reproduction of their

Shakespearean prose

heaven only knows why i'm so inclined to malevolent

adaptations of love

recapitulating the err of their inclination

my life is their story

stuck on repeat

and i loop the best times they spent lost in each other

and the worst times they shared tearing out their

Beautiful Strange

souls in destructive manipulations

to try and ease the pain

so i find no shame in my treacherous tales of lovers

past

for i am a strange adaptation of love's first kiss

and a beautiful reflection of its burn

Jackals In The Night

he told me i was Beautiful

and i'm sure he had no idea

how much it burned

like flaming shears

slicing open poorly stitched wounds

lesions so deep the nerve endings no longer function

spaces Inside of me that will forever be numb

i remember the first time

i was told i was Beautiful as a woman

i recall vividly how it made me feel

bashful and shocked all at the same time

i never knew then

that word would kill the very essence

of all that was me

too many times to know the count

but i can name each and everyone of my murders

each and every man who used that word

Beautiful Strange

to pry open the most sacred parts of me

then ransack the womb of my soul

some of them tiptoed out

once they took their mind's desires

from my storehouse

others left as violently as they came

making sure to smash and break

whatever they were unable to carry

in their large strong arms

nevertheless

they all left

left me there ravished

and bleeding

and bruised

and beaten

and Beautiful

still Beautiful enough

for the next jackal to find me in the darkness of night

Beautiful enough

11

Kalandra St. George

for his nose to be filled

with the scent of blood so strong

his loins were always full

by the time he reached me

and although each time

i was left less than before

there always seemed to be

more beauty

a hellious beacon

whose only purpose

was to attract prowlers continuously to my tomb

so here i lay

lifeless and desecrated

exposed and hopeless

looted and plundered

shattered and torn

exhausted and angry

ashamed and confused

but still

oh so Beautiful

Beautiful Strange

Celibacy

I will not

Lay back & spread my legs

Enticing you

With the scent of my Eve juices

Sent by the swift decent of

'Oh baby please' music

And

'Fuck the condom we don't need to use it'

You wanna climb atop my

Thick curvaceous frame

Housing my

Emotionally scarred brain

And prepare to blow my mind

Plans to make me

Scream your name

As your cock pounds my womb

Bruised from the sounds of Lover's Groove

Marvin Gaye's *Let's Get It On*

Got you in the mood

Kalandra St. George

For sexin'

You stand there and stare

The gleam in your eyes

Larger than your swelled erection

Heading slowly in my direction

Head plump pulsating from what you call affection

I see as violation

Of my

Much needed Well deserved

Long time coming Libation

Which you ignore

Holding in your eager hands

A vicious coagulation

Deaf to my demands

Of Spiritual liberation

Come on baby got damn

What happened to all the patience

You had those times before

The deepest realms of my body

I allowed you to implore

14

Beautiful Strange

Now you sittin here As if I'm wrong

Now you wanna imply

If I refuse to comply

I need to gather my shit And get gone

Cause all you hunger for

Is the sustenance of my nectar

And can't even see my soul Crying for completion

Your only focus

Semen depletion

And creamin' and skeetin' Like dogs in heat

and Ridin' me to ya funky beats

While you grunt and heave Leavin' funky sheets

So you can still smell me the next day

Well dear you must've heard me wrong

Cause we not singin' the same song

And

Ain't no thing for me to move on

And

If my desire ever grows too strong

And

Kalandra St. George

If for release my fire comes to long

Then

Self gratification leaves me with no qualms

Cause

These five extensions of my palm

Always

Keep me nice and warm

And

Bring to me no harm

So

Don't worry brotha

I got this...

Beautiful Strange

Tears

Tears

Salty on my palette

Taste like mangos

Dipped in mustard

Smashed & hammered

With a mallet

Validating the reality

That I truly care

Dissolving under the weight of my tongue

Saliva becomes as thick as despair

Trickling down my cheeks

Leaving molten streaks

Burns

And dry skin marks

Tight face

Tender nose

Resulting from this journey embarked

Upon called love

The cup offering intoxicants

Kalandra St. George

One moment

The next deadly venom

Spills from its mug

Tastes like tears

Precipitated fears

Moist

As they gather around the brim

The liquid inside

Reflect memories of him

His touch

His smell

All of which I know too well

Can't understand

The heaven that's held

In this purgatory

Dreams become jinns'

Making every effort to sully

The image of he that adores me

Cause see I admire him too

And the longer we're apart

Beautiful Strange

The worse off it gets

As in solitude

This meal I consume

Tastes like tears

Dipped in doom

Recalling how once

This table's centerpiece bloomed

Now my chin's fallen amongst expired buds

Offering no beauty to this room

Empty belly a mirror

Of my womb

That now holds nothing more than fallen tears...

Kalandra St. George

Moonmilk

sleeping unclothed

bearing my soul to will of the night

praying the Lord will send His angels of protection to

 camp around me

praying His love will make its way into my nostrils

so that I may inhale His truths

feed my coursing veins

so that I may sustain long enough

to know of which these eyes can't see

but this heart shutters to

if never uttered by these lips

but rather written by this ink

let every drop spill perfectly peaceful

across pages in utter disarray

let these words reach my daughter's tongue

so that she may swallow

the lights she was birthed into

and exhale the moon

with every rise and fall of her breast

Beautiful Strange

keep her O Lord guide her in your mercy

may her nights be filled with heaven's stars

and her days with the splendor of your works...

Kalandra St. George

Southpaw

My right hand is itching

Fire burning

Like oil in the palm of my soul

Berated bridges decorated with flowers

A remembrance of loss suffered in past battles

Some wars are fought whole armies at a time

Others methodically single handed

Bare chested and shield tested

Like the legend of Achilles and got-dammit you're

Hector

Oblivious to the fact that

You've signed your own certificate of death

All the while professing to the heart of the heavens

that you are the hero

Still today my right hand is itching

Fire burning

Like oil in the palm of my soul

And guess what?...

...I'm left handed

22

Beautiful Strange

Relativity

-Relativity is defined as a state of dependence in
which the existence or significance of one entity is
solely dependent on that of another-

not on no still holding on shit
just vibing off relativity
like
is it not relative that i bleed
just like the womb that once
held your seed
wrapped in her blood
from whence came you to be
like
is the tug of
that type love
not what we all need
what we all breathe
or is it not relative
like

Kalandra St. George

is it not relative

that i cried from your words

my pain ignored

so i screamed

thrusting my heart against

your soundproof walls of indifference

while in my misery

you gleam

until i stroke out

like strike out

like

i lose you leave

like

is it not relative

that so once did your mister

and so once did mine

like

can't we be different

and like on the same path

like

Beautiful Strange

at the same time

or is forgiveness not relative

like

is forgiveness not relative

like

were those vows not binding

knots tied with bare fingers reminding

word as bond

like did we not bond

and create a new life from our bond

or is that not relative

like

it being four years later

and i still smell you in my daydreams

like honey against the roof of my mouth

i still taste you say things

like

kiss me until your throat hurts

or is all that sweet shit not relative

like

Kalandra St. George

you turning into a stranger

i happened to know

once upon a time

like the day you told me

you're no relative of mine

then walked away with a grin

like

is it not relative

that i died right then

just like i died a hundred times over

at every mention of your name

like

is it not relative

that i have to call my sun by the same

and strangely it both intensifies

and alleviates the pain

like

is this not insane

or is the love we once had

no longer relative...

26

Beautiful Strange

im not on no still holding on shit....

im just vibing off relativity....

Kalandra St. George

Tennessee

i'd fallen in love with the idea of

crushing you with my sighs

clutching you between my cries

moments in time must all come to an end...

and so it begins

that i thrust to let you go

rush let you blo

from the recesses of my earth

steadily i uncover

the beauty of your nakedness like Georgia's red dirt

still bitter on the tip of my tongue

still stained on the folds of lips which once hung

open for you...

to ultimately become satiated

yet today

with the rising of the sun

i found myself emancipated

freed from fantasies of smelling you in my sleep

28

Beautiful Strange

and instead slow deliberate strokes of its zenith

hushed me to reach

lush green tops of

tennessee mountain peaks

that tremble

without you...

Kalandra St. George

Satin Sheets

Slowly she slips

In between satin sheets

Saturated with sultry sweet scents

That overnight

Have switched to stench

Soliloquies on why

She should stay

While steadily in solitude

Her slumbering supposedly lays

Spiritually separated

She hasn't slept in days

Sometimes it's seems months

Since love stole her sanction then slid away

Forbid away some selfish return

Sparks ignite the steam

Scantily smothered she screams

As this sexuality her soul spurns

Scowling sheep pretend to shiver and weep

Showing slight with concern

Beautiful Strange

Sands of quick offer no sight of return

Shunted symbols of hope

Semantic lines lie like coke

Served to scar the synergy of her nose

Synapsis seared never to again someday compose

The senseless song of love's morose joys

"Should have's" stale and suffocating

Symbolically coy

Still she succumbs to the séance...

Of her satin sheets

Kalandra St. George

Gentleman's Jack

When He Was Sober He Was Silent

A Stone Wall Of Uninterested Being

And He Never Listened

He Always Cut Me Off

Changing The Subject Like Radio Stations

Extinguishing My Airways

Still I Loved Him Through Deaf Tones

When He Was Drunk He Was Obnoxious

Loud And Abrasive

Mouth As Dirty As The Gravel He Bled His Harley

On

And It Was Then That I Found Out That He Listened

He'd Repeat Every Muted Word I'd Ever Spoken

He'd Vow His Heart To My Soul For As Long As His

Lungs Drew Breath

Beautiful Strange

And Through Sweet Stench Of A Whiskey Flavored

Tongue

He'd Spew His Love To The Sky Like Star Dust

And Turn My Head To Face The Night

As His Love Rained On

Kalandra St. George

Lamentations: A Series

Vamping

my soul is covered with passion marks of lovers past

that left me with nothing more than discolorations

along the length of my psyche...

some are deeper than others

a couple hidden from view

even a few on the brink of laceration

and like a fool

i sat perfectly still for each and every one...

allowing them to suck the blood to just beneath my

surface

as if mocking vampires is sexy in real life...

fucking idiot...

White Liquor

stuck inside myself_

trying to find myself_

and i'm gone_

Beautiful Strange

before i even had the chance to arrive_

nevermore had i even the stance to devise_

a glance to surmise_

what i believe to be absoult_

and who am i to tell the thoughts of an inebriated

mind...???...

Lyrics

shapeless memories

forlorn locs of previous lovers

those who never even cared enough to remember her

name

always the same

so she constantly rearranged

fabricated rationalities in her head

the emptiness filled her soul

so instead

she replayed lyrics of her favorite song

letting her subconscious sing sweetly along

Kalandra St. George

while neglected and mutilated her self worth

tragically bled

she heard dying alone was the worst kind of fate...

Beautiful Strange

The Crow and The Butterfly

i hear his squawking so close

it bites the tip of my ear

black in all of his beauty

along side him ive never known fear

for he is a winged stallion

and i the honeydew colored mare

his voice to my essence a medallion

of two oddities that seamlessly pair

calling to the realms

my silence

welcoming in its prose

to the naked eye

appearance unruly

to the understood

a calming for the soul

Kalandra St. George

together we paint existence

like the motion of sediment under waves

our culmination of each other's resistance

joined devotion

set ablaze

when he sees me he bows

and i in his wake

do the same

for i am often called life and him death

neither of which will ever be contained

i come to follow the sun

and float on rays that pierce the breeze

he soars without effort in the seas of the skies floating

 beneath heaven's trees

and it is with this ease that we commune

when beckoned to the will of flight

Beautiful Strange

for no one can resist the squawking of the crow come
death

nor the silent beauty of the butterfly come life.....

Kalandra St. George

I Am Life

I am life

Abrupt and painful

Bloody and blissful

Ill formed in all of its perfect defects

Life

Oceans of tears that create endless rivers of

happiness

Drowning the sorrows of yesterday with each suns

rise

I am life

Rough and rude

Eloquent and understanding

Insightful in all things

Yet oblivious to the obvious truths of reality

Life

Stubborn and insubordinate

Demanding and selfish

Emotional and sensitive

Like the retina to a blaring beam

Beautiful Strange

Screaming at the top of deflated lungs

Gasping from too much air

I am life

Tender and robust

Intricate and inclined

Racing frantically against time unseen

Winded from lack of proper training

Life

Staining and permanent

Temporary and casual

Misunderstood and so well known

Remembered while always forgotten

Desired while never accepted

I am LIFE

Knowledge

i keep a pen in my left hand

can't live as a yes man

i thank God He made me black

so i will forever write

facts that fight back

distortions of histories

until they once again become truth

their ink to my paper

his blood to their hands

my Sun's to these sands

won't stand still

like water froze up

man down

i mean hold up

i mean hands up

nah man up

fists closed Sun

shine

eyes open

Beautiful Strange

"the hardest thing in this world to be is a black Man"

i mean wide open

"whose world is this?"

each time

"the world is yours"

so i will forever preach it

forever teach it

know thy self

until your soul

repeats it

know thy self

and once you

know the ledge

it's nothing to fly ....

My People

Hold on my people like

The grips of ropes around necks so tight

No hope in sight

But we still

Grope and fight

For each chosen life

My people hold on

Hold on my people like

The roots of crooked trees

Branches that couldn't believe

Being used as weapons of atrocities

Lessons of democracies

Make my people hold on

Hold on my people like

Dreams slain to death

By feelings of hate

Seen pain in breaths

Taken to shake shame and fate

But we are destined to be great

Beautiful Strange

My people hold on

Hold on my people like

Arms around your mother's neck

Like left hand palms

Pressed to your lover's left

Like your favorite songs

That saved you from sudden death

Like a place so warm

You could have never guessed

The heat from the sun

Could feel so good

Like the Motherland

Stretched out her arms

And on her soil you stood

Hold on my people

Cause my people will forever

Hold on!

Kalandra St. George
About the Author

Poet and author Kalandra St. George, also known as Kalandra Yvonne lives and dies by her saying "Give m e words or free my soul for both cannot exist". Kalan dra debuted onto the writing stage with "A Turn of K ismet" in 2015, a novel that wraps the reader in a plea sant fog of truth, friendship, pain, love, and desire.

St. George also freelances for local artists in the mu sic industry and has recently e has been tapped as a c o-writer/producer for an upcoming television Hip-Ho p series. She remains very active within her communi ty, and her work extends beyond the realm of the wri tten word. She's delighted audiences as she hosted "T he Black Tour" fashion show at Stitches Design Studi

Beautiful Strange

o in Atlanta, Georgia. Kalandra has lent her voice to s
tand against domestic violence as a volunteer for PA
DV, the Partnership Against Domestic Violence, and
educated youth at the DeKalb County Board of Healt
h Teen Pregnancy Prevention Program: Steps Toward
the Future as a Youth Program Speaker/Instructor.

A prolific author, poet, and community activist, Ka
landra St. George continues to use her experiences to
not only captivate audiences but to instill a sense of s
trength and responsibility in today's youth. She curre
ntly resides in the Metro Atlanta area with her three
beautiful children.

Kalandra St. George

A Turn of Kismet is available on Amazon, Barnes

and Noble and more! For a complete list of retailers

visit www.printhousebooks.com.

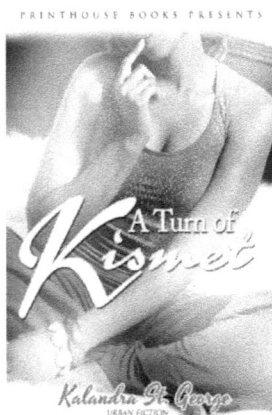

Beautiful Strange

Contact the Author

Follow Kalandra on IG: instagram.com/kalandrayvonne

Visit Kalandra on Twitter: twitter.com/kalandrayvonne

Subscribe to Kalandra's Blog: writ-of-insanity.tumblr.com

Thank you for reading Beautiful Strange by Kalandra St. George. Don't hesitate to leave a review on Amazon or Barnes & Noble comment forums. We would love to hear from you! Please check out more titles at PrintHouseBooks.com

PRINTHOUSEBOOKS.com
Read it! Enjoy it! Tell A Friend!
Atlanta, GA.

Beautiful Strange

Read it! Enjoy it! Tell A Friend!

www.ingramcontent.com/pod-product-compliance
Lightning Source LLC
Chambersburg PA
CBHW021915040426
42447CB00007B/863